SARASWATI VIDMAHE

The Complete English Guide to Vasant
Panchami Saraswati Pooja and Yajna

SHRI SHRAV BANERJEE

ILLUSTRATIONS BY: SHRI SHRAV BANERJEE

SHRI GANESHAYA NAMAH

SHRI SHRI SARASWATWAI NAMAH

*This book is dedicated to Goddess Saraswati who came in
my life and removed all darkness*

Table of Contents

Introduction

Puja/pooja is a way of life. It's how one behaves, performs his/her daily rites, and shows others respect. If done systematically, the prayer of Gods or Goddesses is to be done properly, well-defined as mentioned in Sanatan Dharma's *Vedas, Purans* and *Lok-achar*. Lok-achar is defined in the Vedas as being above them. One should prioritize the culture of their family, i.e. *Kul-achar*, society i.e. *Gramya-achar*, and finally the rules and regulations mentioned in the holy granthas. The importance of Saraswati puja lies in many ways:

1. For a **priest**: Priests achieves immense knowledge and understanding of music and even brahma gyan can be achieved through Saraswati puja
2. For a **common person**: A common person can pray to Saraswati for knowledge gain and fulfilment of short term as well as long term desires.
3. For **teachers and students**: They pray to Saraswati for gain in knowledge and peace of mind.

"Saraswati Vidmahe: The Complete English Guide to Vedic Saraswati Pooja and Yajna" by Shri Shrav Banerjee will introduce you to the deep wisdom and beauty of the worship of Maa Saraswati. It will be a lucid and practical guide for the serious aspirant, for the beginner who is new to the holy traditions, to do Saraswati Puja with sincerity and love.

Saraswati tatwa is one of the most complicated tatwa in Sanatan Dharma. She is one of the primary roopa of Maha Tripura Sundari, she resides on the tongue of a sadhaka (seekers of knowledge). Lets take a quick and short dive in the immense sea of Saraswati tatwa.

Saraswati tatwa

Appearance of Saraswati:

As per Brahmavarta purana, Brahma explains that Devi Mahamaya appeared to him as a beautiful and young girl, seeing the mesmerizing beauty, Brahma fell in love with her and started admiring her. She moved to the back and Brahma grew a head at the back then subsequently his left and right heads grew in the same manner but as soon as he grew his 5th head staring above, Rudra got angry and cut Brahma's 5th head. Realising his mistake, Brahma started immense tapasya for creating something to regain his shakti, Devi guided him to write the Vedas and then she appeared in the form of Saraswati and became his *ardhangini.*

Brahma's curse:

When it was time for creation of nature, Brahma sat for yajna but Saraswati did not came. Brahma asked Ma Mahamaya to bestow him with a woman to marry and perform yajna with Brahma. *Savitri* as a beautiful woman appeared, married Brahma and sat with him in yajna. When Saraswati saw this, she cursed Brahma that he will not be worshipped in his own creation except at some places like pushkar lake.

Saraswati as *Vishnu-priya*:

Saraswati left Brahma and remarried Vishnu, the preserver. This may seem very disturbing but has a literal meaning. Brahma is the creator; one can create anything with knowledge but to preserve a creation one needs both Laxmi (money and discipline) and Saraswati (knowledge and perseverance).

Saraswati Dhyan Mantra

Dhyan Mantra:

Aum taruna shakala mindora bibhrati subhrakantih, kucha-varana mitangi, sanni sanna sitabje| Nijo karo kamaladyo pustaka lekhani shri sakala bibhava siddhou paatu vaag devata naha||

Meaning:

A Young girl (*taruna*) whose fair complexion is like that of half-moon (*shakala mindora*), she is the whitest (*subhrakantih*) of all. Her chest is filled with heavy ornaments (*kucha-varana*) such that she is slightly bending forward (*mitangi*). She is praised by saints (*sanni sanna*) and is seated on white lotus (*sitabje*). She holds in her four hands (*nijo karo*): Lotus (*kamal*), Shruba (*adyo*), Book (*pustaka*) and a beautiful Pen (*lekhani shri*). She is the bestower (*sakala bibhava*) of several gyan and qualities (*siddhou*) in her pujaris. She is the Vaak devi who protects me (*paatu vaag devata naha*).

Importance of this mantra:

A pujari must compulsorily pray to Maa Saraswati with this dhyan mantra before pran pratistha and any puja with kurma mudra and correct spelling and knowing the proper meaning of this mantra.

Questions and Answers

What are the methods of pooja and what method this book focuses on?

Ans. As most people follow Yajur veda and it is the veda that must be followed in all sarvajanin pujas, this book follows Yajur vedic puja of Maa. The author will try to upload the Rig and Shyam Vedic pujas in the following editions.

What is my Veda? And what to do if I do not know my Veda?

Ans. You can know your Veda by asking your elderly people of the house. In any puja of your house, you will have to follow your/your Guru's Veda. In any public/sarvajanin Puja, you will have to follow Yajur Veda. If, you are unable to know your Veda, you can follow Yajur Veda.

Who can perform Puja?

Ans. Anyone with *Bhakti* and knowledge of Puja procedure can easily perform puja and satisfy God.

Can females perform Puja?

Ans. Females are forms of Aadi para-shakti, they can and should perform puja. It is a perception of the author that women can do better pujas than men.

What if my way of chanting mantras is incorrect? How to check that?

Ans. The power of Bhakti and a clean mind is far more than the power of mantras. If you face any doubt in chanting your mantras, feel free to contact your Guru, he/she will show you the right path.

Pre-requisites for a Puja

1. Take a **bath** and wear **clean clothes** like dhoti and uttorio (for males) or saree (for females) and **clean the area** in which Puja will the done

2. The following things are required for puja: **Bedi/seat** for Saraswati, **cloth** to cover the bedi, **siddhi, sindoor, asan** for yourself, **ghanta, rice, chandan, haldi, soil, kush (Darbha) grass** which has to be made into:
I. A ring (**kushangurio**),
II. Taking 3 kush together and tying them with thread to make a **tripatrika**, and
III. Some Kush are to be saved for Yajna,
Panch-sasya: Whole wheat, til, white mustard seed, barley, and mash-korai daal, **white mustard seed** is required separately too, **haritaki** (myrobalan fruit), **achaman patra** (panch patra), **kosha-kushi**/Saman-arghya patra, **jal-sankha**/ Bishesh-arghya sankha, **sankha** for playing, **panch ratna**/ 5 gems, **panch guri**/ Five colours, **kalash** for Ghat and Dwar Ghats, **daab**(Coconut)/banana for Ghat, **tirkathi, red-yellow string, holy thread (*yajnapavita*)** for Saraswati, Narayan and pujari, **panch pallab**: 3, 1 for main ghat and 2 for Dwar ghats, **chand mala-** 1 large for murthi and 1 small for Ghat, **clothes** (5): 1 for Ghat, 1 for Pujari, 1 for Narayan and 1 for Saraswati and 1 for Arati, big handi (**kundo-handi**) with **mirror** for offering puja, **rajat asan** (silver asan for Saraswati), **abhoran**/jewelry for Saraswati, Clean water/Ganga jal, **panch gavya: gomutra, gomaya, milk, dadhi, ghee, madhu, clay patras and plates** for offering food and others, **glass** for offering water, **dry coconut, dhup**/ incense sticks, **deep**/candle, **oil, cotton, paan**/tambul, five types of **fruits, sweets**: laddoo, modak

etc, **garlands**: minimum 4, 1 each for Saraswati, Ghat, Laxmi, and Narayan, **flowers**: as per requirement and must be mixed with **chandan, durba, bilwa patra**: As per requirement, **karpoor** with **kapoor stand, panch-deep, hand-fan/chamar** for arati, things to be put in the thali for welcoming Saraswati through **Adhivas** puja:
Patra with some **soil, chandan**, small **stone, rice, durba, flower, fruit, curd, ghee, swastik/shri** (a cone-like structure made with powdered rice), **sindoor**, small **sankha, kajal, haldi, white mustard seeds, ornaments, hand-fan/chamar, darpan**/mirror, **deep, mangal sutra** made with durba tied in a red-yellow string.

3. **Gifts for pujari** if you are doing puja for others

4. **Cover the asan** of Saraswati with red cloth, spread **rice** on the asan and place the **Saraswati murthi/photo/yantra** over it facing him towards **west** (preferable) or south, put books and stationary items (*kalam -doat*). Give a **lotus, Mustard flowers** and **muscial instrument** in her hands.

Fig. Sarvata-Bhadra Mandal

5. Prepare the **Ghat**: **Tie** the Ghat with string and Durba, draw the **Sarvata-bhadra mandal** on the ground with panch guri, place a ladden of **soil (preferably Ganga mati)** in its centre, sprinkle **panch sashya, panch guri, siddhi, and rice** and place the kalash over it. Fill the kalash with water, put **panch ratna, haldi, sindoor, panch sasya and panch-pallab** in it. Put a **shora/patra filled with rice** over the kalash and place a **paan** leaf and the **daab**/coconut over it. **Apply sindoor** to the ghat, **cover it** with a cloth and give the ghat a **garland**.
Make **4** ladden masses of soil, keep at four corners of the ghat and put one **tir-kathi** in them. Tie the tips of the tir-kathi with **red-yellow string** so that the Gods and Goddesses are tied in the Ghat and within the four Vedas.

6. Make the **Pushpa-patra** ready. Keep the following it it: **Flowers** pre-mixed with chandan, **garlands, chandan**, small patra with **honey, panch-sasya, white mustard, kushangurio, tripatrika, haldi, sindoor.**

7. Keep the things required for arati ready: **Panch-deep, karpoor with stand, incense sticks, jal-sankh, flowers, one cloth, hand fan.**

8. Light ghee/oil **diya** on the left side of Saraswati and **incense sticks** on her right side.

9. Keep image/murthi of **Laxmi Narayan** besides Saraswati,

10. Fill **dwar ghat** kalash with water, place panch-pallab in it and a fal (daab/haritoki) on it. Apply sindoor and keep them outside the door,

11. Enter the room of puja with **left** foot first,

12. Prepare the **naivedya** for Saraswati: In a clean plate put rice, mix with clean water, put some sweets and fruits on it, never give Banana to Maa Saraswati.

13. Sit on the asan and **fill up achaman patra** with clean water, and

14. Now, we are ready to start the puja.

Note:

1. As this book is for public use, the whole puja and yajna vidhi has no mention of **Saraswati beej mantra**. The beej mantra is given by a guru to shisya. Those who know the beej mantra of Saraswati can use the beej mantra before every name of Saraswati otherwise, puja can also be done without the beej mantra.

2. The **specific Gayatri** of Saraswati is: *Saraswati Vidmahe Brahmaputri dheemahi tanno devi prachodayat| Aum Padapada baag-vaadini devi Saraswattai namaha|*

3. **NOT** every part of this book have to be blindly followed by the reader. They must follow their Kul and Gramya achars and also the way directed by their Guru. They must use this book as a reference for modifying/learning the basics of Saraswati Puja and Yajna.

4. If one is unable to collect all the things required for puja, its not of any problem as all Shastras direct devotees to do the puja as per their **samarth/ capability**.

5. All the *mantras* are italicised and **important points** bolded for the ease of the pujari.

Shri Shri Saraswati Puja Vidhi

Achaman

Clean both hands with some water, drop a pinch of water in your right hand and drink it from the proximal border of your palm, then again clean your right hand with water and again take a small amount of water to sprinkle on your umbilicus, back, shoulder, elbow, hands, lips, both the nostrils, eyes, ears, and top of your head. Wash both hands and now chant:

Aum Vishnu Aum Vishnu Aum Vishnu||

Vishnu smaran

Join your hands in namaskar mudra and chant:

Aum tat Vishnu paramam padam sada pashyanti suraya dibibo chakshuratatam| Namo Vishnu Namo Vishnu Namo Vishnu||

Aum aapavitra pabitraba sarbavastang gato-pibah yatsmarent pundorikakshyang sa bajjyah abhyantaro suchi| Namo Suchi Namo Suchi Namo Suchi||

Aum sarbamangalya mangalye varenyang varadang subham Narayanam namaskrittyam sarba karmani karoyet|

Aum sankham chakram dharang Vishnung dwibhujang pitabasasam| Prarambhe karmana bipram pundorikang smare dhaare||

Aum Madhava Madhava bachi Madhava Madhava hridi smaranti sadhavak sarbe sarva su karyeshu Madhavam| Shri Madhavam Shri Madhavam Shri Madhavam||

Aum papaham papakarmahang papadam pundorikashyang sarba karye haro hari| Aum Shri Hari Aum Shri Hari Aum Shri Hari||

Mangalam bhagwan Vishnu mangalam garura dhwajah mangalam pundorikashyong mangaloi su magalam||
Now, do Ganesh, Guru, Panch-devata, Agni Pithodevata, Adityadi Navagraha, Indradi dashdikpal, Matsyadi dashavatar, Kaliadi Dashmahavidya, Vastu dev-devi, Kula dev-devi, Ishtha dev-devi with gandhapushpa like: *Ete gandhapushpe Ganeshaya namaha...*

Tilak dharan

This mantra has been used by several rishis of ancient times to wear tilak, say this mantra and mark a tripunda on your head with haldi:
Sadyojat Mantra:

Aum Sadyojaatam prapadyami sadyo jataajava namo namaha| Bhaave Bhavenaati Bhave Bhavasvamaam Bhavodbhavay Namaha||
Mark a red tilak in the centre of the tripunda with is mantra:
Vamdeva Mantra:

Aum Vamdevay namaha Jeshthaya namaha Shreshthaya namaha Rudraya namaha Kaalaye namaha Kaala vikranaaye namaha Balavikranaye namaha Balaye namaha Bala paramathanaaye namaha Sarvabhoota damanaye namaha Manonanaaye namaha|

Kush-angurio dharan

Ring made with kush is worn in **right ring finger** with this mantra to invoke the brahmin in you:
Devetat prakittam chittan papakranto mahabhunanam. Tannihi sarayo papang hung fatt cha te namaha| Aum Suryayo Shomo Yamo Kaalo Maha Bhutanani pancho cho| Ete subha ashubhoshyo karmeno shakshino nabo||

Ghanta Puja

Sprinkle water on ghanta three times with mantra:
Aum jayadhwani mantra matayo swaha|

Flower: *Ete gandhapushpe Aum sarba badyamayo jayadhwani mantra matayo namaha|*

Suryargho daan

Take durba, chandan, red flower, rice, water, panch-shashya, til in a kushi and chant:
Aum ehi Suryah sahastraksho tejorashe jagatpate| Anukampaya mang bhaktang grihan arghyam Divakaram| Edam arghyam Aum namo bhagawate Suryayo namo||

Give the arghya to Surya and then pranam: *Aum japa kusuma sankhashang kashyapiyang maha-dhutim dhwantarim sarva papaghang pranohtashming Divakarm|*

Swastivachan

Fill kushi with rice, close it and chant:
Aum kartabhehasmin subha Shri Shri Ganeshadi nanadevata puja purbak Saraswati Puja karmani| Aum purnahang bhavantu bhrubantu Aum purnahang bhavantu bhrubantu Aum purnahang bhavantu bhrubantu| Aum Purnahang Aum Purnahang Aum Purnahang||
Aum kartabhehasmin Subha Shri Shri Ganeshadi nanadevata puja purbak Saraswati Puja karmani Aum Swasti bhavantu bhrubantu Aum Swasti bhavantu bhrubantu Aum Swasti bhavantu bhrubantu| Aum Swasti Aum Swasti Aum Swasti||

Aum kartabhehasmin Subha Shri Shri Saraswati Puja karmani Aum Hriddhi bhavantu bhrubantu Aum Hriddhi bhavantu bhrubantu Aum Hriddhi bhavantu bhrubantu| Aum Hriddhyatam Aum Hriddhyatam Aum Hriddhyatam||

Spread the rice along with playing ghanta:

Aum swastina Indra briddhashravaha, Swastina pusha biswavedaha| Swastina sakshyat aaristonemih swastina Brihaspatir dadhatu|| Aum Swasti Aum Swasti Aum Swasti||

Swasti sukta:
Put kushi in front and chant with ghanta:

Aum Gananang twa Ganapatevyo hawamahe, Aum Priyanang twa priyapatebhyo hawamahe, Aum Nidhinang twa nidhinapatebhyo hawa mahe baso mamaha||
Aum Swasti Aum Swasti Aum Swasti||

Sakshyo

This mantra invokes the 5 mahabhut who are the witnesses of all your actions, chant with namaskar mudra:

Aum Surayah Shomo Yamo Kaalo Sandhye Mahabhutanang panchacho shava bhabhano dikpalyeter bhumire akasho khaschara amara brindya| Brahmang shashanang asthaya kalpa dwam yaha sannidhim||

Chant *Gayatri* mantra at least 10 times.

Sankalpa

In kosha-kushi or panchpatra keep panch-shashya, rice, any fruit (except betel nut), flower etc. and sit facing north with right knee touching the ground and left above (with your holy thread in hand- if you have one), touch the fruit and say the **sankalpa vakya:**

Aum Vishnurang tatsad adyo <month, tithi according to Saka calendar> <Purohits' names with gotra> (karoyet <beneficiary name with gotra> mot sankalpito) Shri shri Saraswati priti kaamo ebang gyan vriddhihetu puja karmahang <korishyami- for others/korishye- for yourself>|

For example, if one is doing the Vasant panchami puja for themself, then they would say:

Aum Vishnurang tatsad adyo Maagh mashe Sukle pakshe Panchamo tirthou Shri Shrav Banerjee Shandilya gotra Shri shri Saraswati priti kaamo o gyan vriddhi-hetu puja karmahang korishyami|

Sankapla sukta: Provide the fruit to the Saraswati and say:

Aum yajjagrata dura-mudaiti devim tathaubati tauthou bashya durgama jyotishyang jyoti rekhang tanme mann Shiva sankalpa matsyu| Aum aayam arombhya subharambhya asya sankalpito rasya asya siddhi dhaarastu||

Gandha dravya archana

Sprinkle water on flowers and chandan and say: *Bong etoshmoing gandha dravyay namo|*
Give **flower** on it: *Ete gandhapushpe gandha dravyay namo| Etot adhipataye devaya Shri Vishnobay namo|*
Give a **flower to Saraswati**: *Sampradanaya gandha dravya Aum Saraswattai namah||*

Pujari baran

This is done when you will be praying for yajman. The yajman would give you a cloth, yajnopavita (Holy thread), flowers, fruits, garland, and money in a plate and say that he/she will be unable to perform the puja on his/her own, so would request you to do the puja after accepting the gifts in their regional language. You will also have to accept the gifts, promise that you will do the puja as per your knowledge and continue with the puja.

Gurupankti puja

Show namaskar and direct hands to the side mentioned:

Left: *Vaame Aum gurbhye namaha,*
Right: *Dakshine Aum Ganapataye namaha,*
Above: *Urdhe Aum Brahmanye namaha,*
Down: *Aadhe Aum Anantaye namaha,*
Back: *Paschate Aum Kshetrapalaye namaha,*
Ghat: *Sarba mandala maddhye Aum Shri Narayanaya namaha,*
Front: *Samanne Aum Saraswattai namaha|*

Panchagavya

As per Vedas these 5 gavyas are the best way to make everything *pavitra*, these are to be kept in a bowl separately with a kush and mixed at last.

Gomutra: Chant *Gayatri* mantra.
Gomaya: *Aum Gandhadwarang duradrastang nitya pushtang korishinim eshwaring sarbabhutanam tammohipo paheshriyam|*
Milk: *Aum apayeshva sametute biswatwya soma brishnyam bhava bajashya sanghate namah|*
Dadhi: *Aum Dadhi krabno akarishyang jishnurong shasya bajinoh surovino mukhokarat prona ayushi tarikshoyot|*
Ghee: *Aum tejohsi sukramosyo mritomasi dhamana masi priyang debonamo nadrishtang deb janmanamasi|*
Kush: *Aum deboshyo tashobituh prasabehaswi nobbo bahubhyang pushno hastabhya madade|*
Mix: *Gayatri* mantra.

Spread in all ten directions starting from you with the kush.

Narayan snan

Pour water on Narayan, who is the pramukh devta of the puja with this mantra:
Aum sahashra sirsha purushaha shashrakshya shahashrapath sha bhumi biswatto britwa attatishtha dashangulam. Edam snanio Aum Shri Vishnave Narayanaya Namaha|
Wipe Narayan with cloth and place him in his place.

Adhivas puja

Touch each item of the arati-patra/barandala on head of Saraswati murthi, touch the ground and keep them back

Soil: *Aum bhuroshi bhumiroshyo ditiroshi biswodhyaya biswaswa bhubanashya dhatri prithibing gaccho prithibi gung drigung hoh prothibinh ma-hi gung shing| Aum anaya majhya asya Shri Saraswati subhadhivasan mastyu|*

Chandan: *Aum Gandhadwarang duradrastang nitya pushtang korishinim eshwaring sarbabhutanam tammohipo paheshriyam| Aum anaya gandhena asya Shri Saraswati subhadhivasan mastyu|*

Shila/stone: *Aum pra parbatasya brishabhasya prishthanna bashcharanti swasich eyanah| Aum anaya shilaya asya Shri Saraswati subhadhivasan mastyu|*

Dhaan/rice: *Aum dhania masi dhinuhi devan dhinuhi yajnang dhinuhi yajnapating dhinuhi maanang dhinuhi| Aum anenya dhanyena asya Shri Saraswati subhadhivasan mastyu|*

Durba: *Aum kandat kandat parohani purusho purushompori| Ebano durbe pratanu sahashrena shatencha|| Aum anenya durbe asya Shri Saraswati subhadhivasan mastyu|*

Flower: *Aum shrishcho te laxmischo patnya bahoratre parshbe nakshatrani rupmashbinnou byattam| Eshnunni shana musma eeshan, sarvalaxammo eeshan|| Aum anenya pushpena asya Shri Saraswati subhadhivasan mastyu|*

Fruit: *Aum yaha falinya afala apushpa yascha pushpining, Brihaspati prasuta sthano muchonto guhong hangsha| Aum anenya falena asya Shri Saraswati subhadhivasan mastyu|*

Curd: *Aum dadhi krabno akarishyang jishnurong shoshyo bajinoh surovino mukhokarat proh noh ayushi tarikshoyot| Aum anenya dadhna asya Shri Saraswati subhadhivasan mastyu|*

Ghee: *Aum tejohashi sukromosshya mritomasi dhamana masi priyang devanamo nadrishtang deva janmanamasi| Aum anenya ghrita asya Shri Saraswati subhadhivasan mastyu|*

Swastik/shri: *Aum swastina Indra briddhashravaha, Swastina pusha biswavedaha| Swastina sakshyat aaristonemih swastina Brihaspatir dadhatu|| Aum anenya swastikena asya Shri Saraswati subhadhivasan mastyu|*

Sindoor: *Aum sindooribo pradbone sughnonaasho bathpromi yaha patyanti yabaha ghritashya dhara ashruho nah baji kashtaha bhindonong nurmibhiha pinbomanaha| Aum anenya sindoora asya Shri Saraswati subhadhivasan mastyu|*

Sankha: *Aum pratisrutokaya artanang ghoshay vashmantay baahubadin mannantay mukhaghu sabdhaya dambara ghaatmahse binapadang kroshay trina bandham aborsporay
daabopang| Aum anenya shankhena asya Shri Saraswati subhadhivasan mastyu|*

Kajol: *Aum samiddho anjanag kudhorang yatinang ghritamagne madhumat pinboman bahubajinong jaatobedang debenang bakshi priya ma sadhatstham| Aum anenya kajjolena asya Shri Saraswati subhadhivasan mastyu|*

Haldi: *Aum yugnante bradhnamarush paritasthayah rochanante rochana dibi| Aum anenya rochanaya asya Shri Saraswati subhadhivasan mastyu|*

White mustard seeds: *Aum anenya siddhyartha asya Shri Saraswati subhadhivasan mastyu|*

Gold ornament: *Aum anenya kanchanena asya Shri Saraswati subhadhivasan mastyu|*

Silver ornament: *Aum anenya roupena asya Shri Saraswati subhadhivasan mastyu|*

Copper material: *Aum anenya tamrena asya Shri Saraswati subhadhivasan mastyu|*

Fan for Saraswati: *Aum bato ba mano ba gandharbaha saptabiguushati| Te agre sayugnate aasmigyabama dadhuh|| Aum anenya chamorena asya Shri Saraswati subhadhivasan mastyu|*

Darpan/mirror: *Aum anenya darpanena asya Shri Saraswati subhadhivasan mastyu|*

Deep: *Aum agni jyoting rabi jyotish chandra jyoti swathoibo cho jyotischang uttama deva deepayang prati grihajjang| Aum anenya deepang asya Shri Saraswati subhadhivasan mastyu|*

Full aratri patra: *Aum pratipadosi pratipade twa nupadasya nupaade twa sampradasi sampade twa tejohasi tejoshe twa| Aum anenya prashasti patrena asya Shri Saraswati subhadhivasan mastyu|*

Mangalya sutra: *Aum Gananang twa ganapatevyo hawamahe, Aum Priyanang twa priyapatebhyo hawamahe, Aum Nidhinang twa nidhinapatebhyo hawa mahe baso mamaha|| Aum anenya mangalya sutrena asya Shri Saraswati subhadhivasan mastyu|*

Tie the mangal sutra in the right hand of Saraswati.

Saman argha sthapan

Saman arghya is done to sprinkle water from it to provide things to Saraswati. Without the sprinkling of Saman arghya jal, the Gods do not accept any offerings. To form the saman arghya do the following:

Draw a triangle on ground with water (Base of the triangle should face Saraswati), then draw a circle around the triangle and a square around the circle.

Put gandha pushpa on it and chant:

Ete Gandha pushpe Aum Adharsattaye namaha
Ete Gandha pushpe Aum Kurmaye namaha
Ete Gandha pushpe Aum Pritthibo namaha

Ete Gandha pushpe Aum Anantaye namaha|

Put the kosha on the centre, fill with Ganga jal by chanting *"fatt"* mantra, put panch sashya, rice, kush tripatrika and flower in it and chant:

Yoni Mudra

Ete Gandha pushpe Aum Arkamandalaye dwadash kalatmane namaha,
Ete Gandha pushpe Aum Shommandalaye shorosh kalatmane namaha,
Ete Gandha pushpe Aum Banhi mandalaye dasha kalatmane namaha|

Ankush Mudra

Show **avaganthan, yoni mudra** and touch water with **ankush mudra**, and chant:
Aum Gangecho Yamune choibo Godavari Saraswati Narmade Sindhu Karveri Jalehasmin sannidhim kuru|

Now join your hands and chant:

Aum Kurukshetra Gaya Ganga Prabhasa Puskaranicha etabhi tahi punyani Snana kale bhawantiha|

Vishesh argha sthapan

Vishesh arghya means the special gift you would give to Saraswati. It is to be placed in a sankha and well decorated. There are some steps to form the Vishesh arghya:

Draw a triangle on ground with water whose apex is facing towards devi (opposite of Saman arghya),

then draw a circle around the triangle and a square around the circle.

Put gandha pushpa on it and chant:

Ete Gandha pushpe Aum Adharsattaye namaha
Ete Gandha pushpe Aum Kurmaye namaha
Ete Gandha pushpe Aum Pritthibo namaha
Ete Gandha pushpe Aum Anantaye namaha|

Put jal-sankha on flower and fill with Ganga jal by chanting "*fatt*" mantra. Put panch sashya, rice, kush and flower in it and chant:

Ete Gandha pushpe Aum Arkamandalaye dwadash kolatmane namaha
Ete Gandha pushpe Aum Shommandalaye shodash kolatmane namaha
Ete Gandha pushpe Aum Banhi mandalaye dasha kalatmane namaha|

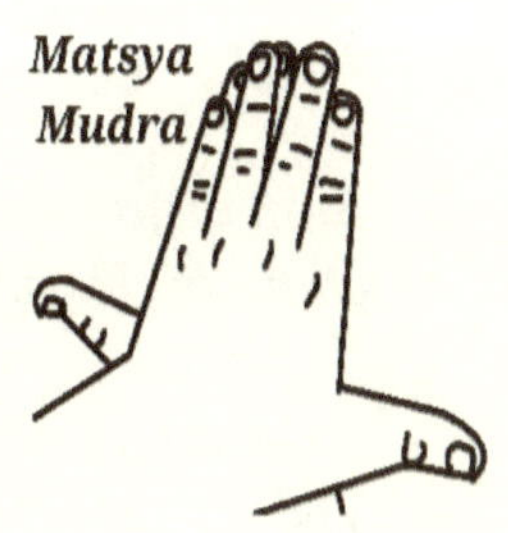

Show **avaganthan, yoni, dehnu, matsya mudra**, and touch water with **ankush mudra**, and chant:

Aum Gangecho Yamune choibo Godavari Saraswati Narmade Sindhu Karveri Jalehasmin sannidhim kuru|

Mix the water of Samanargha and Vishesh argha.

Pushpa suddhi

Flowers must be mixed with chandan. Touch them and say:

Aum pushpe pushpe maha pushpe su pushpe, pushpa shambhabe, pushpachaya bakirnecha hang fatt swaha|

Spread samanargha jal on pushpa and chant:

Pushpaketu Raja hasthe sattyo smmukho somoddhyayo hang|

Offer a flower to Saraswati.

Asan suddhi

Draw a triangle on ground with base towards Saraswati (like samanargha), put gandha pushpa on it and chant:

Ete Gandha pushpe Aum Adharsattaye namaha
Ete Gandha pushpe Aum Kurmaye namaha
Ete Gandha pushpe Aum Pritthibo namaha
Ete Gandha pushpe Aum Anantaye namaha|

Cover the pushpa with asan and touch asan and chant:

Aum asya asana mantrashya meru prishto rishi Sutalang chandou Kurma devata ashan e probeshani viniyogha|

Pranam: *Aum Prithwi twaya dhrita loka devi twaya Vishnu aadrita tancha dharaya mang nityam pavitram kuruchasano|*

Dwar devata puja

Sprinkle saman arghya water on the door: "*Fatt*" mantra. Then touch the top of door with flower and water: *Ete gandha pushpe Aum dwar urdha devata Ganapataye Namaha.*

Give jal and pushpa to the Ghat.

Pranam: *Aum tat-asya jala pushpascha pujaye dwar devatagaan Ganeshang Kshetrapalancho Bakuta Vastupurusha Yogining tatha Gangecho Yamune choibo Laxmi Vaani tatha yatet|*

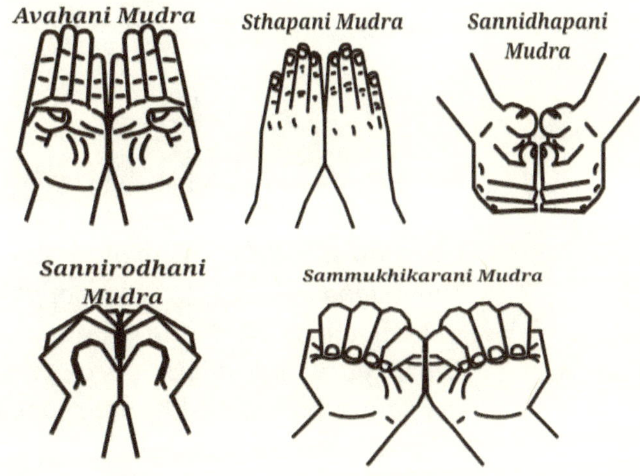

Fig. Avahan-aadi panch mudra

Guru Puja

Call the Gurus: This mantra should be chanted with avahan aadi panch mudras:

Aum Gum Divyougha Siddhougha manabougha Shri Guru Manabo Guru paro gurybhyo paro paro gurybhya Parameshti gurybhya Gurugan eha gacchata eha gacchata (Avahani mudra), *eho tishtata eho tishtata*

(Sthapani mudra), *eha sannidhatto* (Sannidhapani mudra), *eha sannidhrudhyasya* (Sannirodhani mudra), *eho sammukhibhawa* (Sammukhikarani mudra)|

Dhyan: Any dhyan mantra must be chanted with utmost devotion, respect and thinking of the form of dev/devi you are invoking. Take flower, chandan, bilwa patra in Kurma mudra, think of your guru coming to your puja and chant:

Aum brahmanandang parama sukhadang kevalam gyan murthim dwandatitang gagana sadrishang tatya masyadi lakshyam| Ekam nityam bimalam chalang sarbadhi sakshi-bhutang bhabatitang triguna rahitang sat guru twam namami||

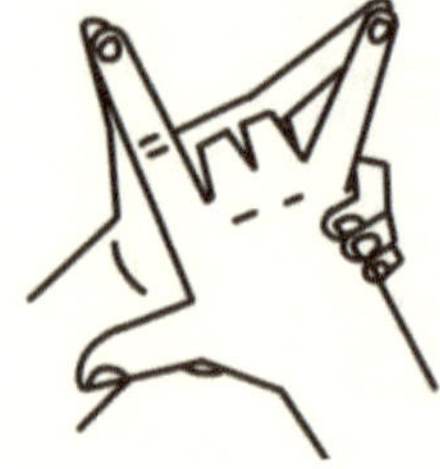

Kurma Mudra

Do puja in Ghat with panch upachar:

Chandan: *Esho Gandha Aum Divyougha Siddhougha manabougha Shri Guru Manabo Guru paro gurybhyo paro paro gurybhya Parameshti gurybhya Gurugane namaha|*

Flower: *Etong Pushpang Aum Divyougha Siddhougha manabougha Shri Guru Manabo Guru paro gurybhyo paro paro gurybhya Parameshti gurybhya Gurugane namaha|*

Rice: *Etot akshata naivedyam Aum Divyougha Siddhougha manabougha Shri Guru Manabo Guru paro gurybhyo paro paro gurybhya Parameshti gurybhya Gurugane namaha|*

Dhup: *Esho dhupam Aum Divyougha Siddhougha manabougha Shri Guru Manabo Guru paro gurybhyo* *paro paro gurybhya Parameshti gurybhya Gurugane namaha|*

Deep: *Esho deepam Aum Divyougha Siddhougha manabougha Shri Guru Manabo Guru paro gurybhyo paro paro gurybhya Parameshti gurybhya Gurugane namaha||*

Pranam (in namaskar mudra): *Aum Gurur Brahma Gurur Vishnu Gurur devo Maheshwara Guru shakshat Parabrahma tasmain Shri Guruve namaha||*

Bhuta suddhi

Spread water around you with *"Rng"* mantra and imagine yourself surrounded by fire and say with namaskar mudra:

Aum mulasringatacchira sushumna pathena jibo Shivang parama Shiva paade yojayaami swaha| Aum yng linga sharirang shoshaya shoshaya swaha| Aum rng shankocha sharirang daha daha swaha| Aum parama shiba sushumna pathena mula shringat mullo-sallos jwala jwala prajjwala prajjwala hang sah Soham swaha||

Hit the floor with left heel 3 times and click 3 times in the air with right hand. Then in pranam mudra:

Aum betalasya, pisachasya, rakshasasya, sarishripa upasarantu sarve Chandika astrena taritaha|

Then spread white mustard seeds all around you as if to scare the ghosts and demons.

Nyash

Kara naysh: Rub index with thumb, then thumb with index, middle, ring and little finger respectively and then clap along with these mantras:

Aum angushtabhyang namaha, Aum tarjanibhyang swaha, Aum Madhyamyang basath, Aum anamikabhyang hung, Aum kanishtabhyang boushat. Aum karatala astraya fatt|

Anga nyash: Touch over the heart, top of head, sikha, opposite shoulders, point towards your 3 eyes and clap respectively with mantra:

Aum hridayay namo, Aum shiroshe swaha, Aum sikhayoi basat, Aum kavachaya hung, Aum netratraya boushat, Aum karatala astraya fatt|

Matrika nyash: Touch top of head, lips, heart, back, thigh, whole body with tatta mudra in both hands and say:

Tatwa Mudra

Aum Prajapati rishoy namaha, Aum Gayatri chondoshyo namaha, Aum matrika Saraswattai namaha, Aum halabhye bijobhye namaha, Aum sarvange matrikaoi namaha, Aum avataroi Kilokaloi namaha|

Rishyadi nyash: Same process of Matrika nyash but the mantras are different:

Aum shirase Brahma rishoy namaha, Aum mukhe Gayatri chondoshyo namaha, Aum hridaye Saraswati devi namaha, Aum Halabhye bijobhye namaha, Aum sarvange Saraswattai namaha, Aum Avataroi Brahmanibhya namaha|

Karosuddhi

Rub flower on palms and say mantra:- *Aum astraya fatt|*
and throw towards Eshaan (North-East) direction.

Dikvandana

Snap your finger in all 10 directions. This is done to show
respect to the devatas of all 10 directions.

Pranayam

7 times breathe in and out though each nose alternatively
with remembering the name/beej mantra of Saraswati while
inspiration.
Manas Puja:- Without saying a word and eyes closed think
of Saraswati in mind for sometime.

Bedi sodhan

To make the asan of Saraswati pavitra, take saman arghya
water and bilvapatra and spread in on the asan and say:
*Aum Bedya bedi somapotte bohishya bohira indrang
jupeno jupo appatyang pronitognina|*

Bitan sodhan

If there is an umbrella/chatri upon Saraswati, take water,
panchgavya and bilvapatra and spread above it and say:
*Aum urdha ushuna udaye tishta devo nah sobitah urdhyo
bajoshyo sabita shadanjibhirbo bhagarbhi havayamahe|*

Pith puja

Call the pith devata in the sarvatobhadra mandal with
avahan-aadi panch mudra:

Aum pitho devatagan eha gacchata eha gacchata, eho tishtata eho tishtata, eha sannidhatto, eha sannidhrudhyasya, eho stithani|

Gandha pushpe puja: *Ete Gandhapushpe Aum Pithodevata ganebhyo namaha|*

Ghat sthapan

Touch the components of the Ghat with durba in hand and say:

Soil: *Aum bhuroshi bhumiroshyo ditiroshi biswodhyaya biswaswa bhubanashya dhatri prithibing gaccho prithibi gung drigung hoh prothibinh mahi gung shing|*

Dhan: *Aum dhanya-masi dhinuhi deban dhinuhi yajnang dhinuhi yajnapating dhinuhi maanang dhinuhi|*

Kalash: *Aum ajighra kalashang mahatyo bishonti bondoboha punor urja nibortoshyo sanoha sahasra dukhyobhyo rudhara payeshwari punorma bishtadriyangha|*

Water: *Aum Varuna shakta vanamasi, Varunashya skombho sarjonisthoha, Varunashya hrito sadanyashi, Varunashya hrito sadanmashi, Varunashya hrito sadanmasidh|*

Pallab: *Aum dhanvanaga dhanvanajing jayem, dhanvana tibraha samdo jayame| Dhanuha shatarupa kamang krinati, dhanbana sarbaha pradisho jayem||*

Fal: *Aum yaha falinya afala apushpo yascha pushpining, Brihaspati prasuta sthano muchonto guhong hangsha|*

Bastra: *Aum juba subashang paribito, agrat sauu shreyan bhavati jaymanaha| Twang dhirasha kabay unnoyanti manasa devayanta||*

Sindoor: *Aum sindoribo pradbane sughnonasho bathpromi yaha patyanti yabaha ghritashya dhara ashruh nah baji kashtaha bhindonong nurmibhiha pinbomanaha|*

Durba: *Aum kandat kandat parohani purusho purushompori| Ebano durbe pratanu sahashreno shatencha||*

Pushpa: *Aum shrishcho te laxmischa patna bahorate parshbe nakshatrani rupam swinou byaktom ishon eshan mummo sharba lakshammo eshanang|*

With 2 hands: Jaap **specific Gayatri** mantra.

Pranam: *Aum sarbatirthod vang baring sarba debo samanwitam, emang ghatam samarujjho tishto debgono shaha|*

Kandoropan/Tir kathi around ghat: *Aum kandat kandat parohani purusho purushompori| Ebano durbe pratanu sahashrena shatencha||*

Sutrobeshton/thread: *Aum sutra manang prithibing dyamneha shang sushman maditi supro niting, Devang nabang swaritram naago samashra banti maruhema swastaye|*

Pran pratistha

Pran pratishta should be done in a closed room with only purohits.

Dhyan of Saraswati: must be done in kurma mudra with flowers, bilvapatra, chandan etc and alongside thinking of the attire of Saraswati:

Aum taruna shakala mindora bibhrati subhrakantih, kucha-varana mitangi, sanni sanna sitabje| Nijo karo kamaladyo pustaka lekhani shri sakala bibhava siddhou paatu vaag devata naha||

and give those to Saraswati.

Call Saraswati with Avahan aadi panch mudra: *Aum bhur bhuba swa swarna Saraswati devi eha gaccha eha gaccha* (Avahani mudra), *eho tishta eho tishta* (Sthapani mudra), *eha sannidha* (Sannidhapani mudra), *eha sannidhatta* (Sannirodhani mudra), *eho sammukhibhawa* (Sammukhikarani mudra), *atradhistang kuru mamah puja grihanang|*

Bang mantra: show **dhenu** mudra

Aum deveshi bhakti sulabhe paribara samanwite| Yaabatyang pujishyami tavatmam su sthira bhawa|

Chakshudaan: Kajal is made by heating ghee on bilwa patra and touched on devi eyes.

Urdha/divya: *Aum kaayanash chitta aabhubha durti saada briddha sakha| Kaaya shachrista brita|*

Left: *Aum chitram debanam udga danikang chakshu mitrasya barunosyagne aapra-drabya prithibing antariksha jagatastha sthu shashthaha|*
Right: *Aum apayesha sametute bishwattoh somo brishyam| bhaba bajasya sangathe|*

Pran pratistha:
Take kush, tripatra, pushpa, swetchandan, atop chaal in right hand and keep it on the head of murthi with 108 times: *Aum Ganapataye namaha* mantra.

Tatwa mudra: keep on heart of Saraswati with atop chal
Aum Aang hring krong yang rang lng bang shang shhang sang houng hang saha Sri sri Saraswati prana eho pranaha|
Aum Aang hring krong yang rang lng bang shang shhang sang houng hang saha Sri sri Saraswati jibo eho stitaha|
Aum Aang hring krong yang rang lng bang shang shhang sang houng hang saha Sri sri Saraswati sarvendrani eho stitani|
Aum Aang hring krong yang rang lng bang shang shhang sang houng hang saha Sri sri Saraswati shotra ghrana prana ehagatto sukhang chirang tishthantu swaha|

Touch the Feet of Saraswati with lelihan mudra:

Lelihan Mudra

Aum manojyoti jushotama jasya brihaspatir yajna mimang tano twarishthang |
Yajna samimang dadhatu, bishwe debas ehoi maadyanta momoh pratishta||

Pranam: *Aum aswai pranah pratishthantu, Aum aswai pranah kharantu cha| Aswai debottwa sankhaoi swaha||*

Vishnu naam jap for 9 times
Maha mrityunjay mantra: *Aum trayambakam yajamahe sugandim pushtim bardhanam urvakrukumeva bandanam mityur mokshi mamritam|*

Chant normal gaytri and specific gayatri|
Do pran pratishtha arati with karpoor|

Dhyan and Avahan:-
Chant the **dhyan mantra** of Saraswati in kurma mudra again with flower and bilwa patra in hand. After dhyan, keep some flower upon your head and and give other to the feet of the lord.
Call Saraswati with water in hand and say:

Aum yatshodarshang michonti devim shobistho siddhoye tasmain te param aisharyo sagatam suswasgatam swagatan chame| Aum kritartho honu grihata hasmin safala jibono momoh, Agoto debo debeshe sushwagatang medong bopu| Aum bhur bhubha swaha Swarna Saraswati swaparibarahoi swabahonaoi swagonaoi swagatang sushwagatang kushalang kuru||

Give jal to ghat and play ghanta.

Pancha devata puja

Process: Dev/devi are thought with the dhyan mantra where your breath is transferred into the flower held in kurma mudra of the hands forming the soul of the dev/devi. Now they are called with their parivar and ganas with avahan aadi pancha mudra. Then puja is done with **panch upachar:**

1. Esho gandho 2. Etong pushpang 3. Esho dhupang 4. Esho dheepang 5. Edom achomonio 6. Eto naivedyam 7. Edom punorachomonio.

Or **dash upachar**:

1. Etong padyang 2. Edam arghyam 3. Edom achomonio 4. Edong snanio jalang 5. Edom achomonio 6. Edong snanio jalang 7. Esho gandho 8. Etong pushpang 10. Esho dheepang 11.Esho dhupang 12. Eto naibedyam 13. Edang panarthodokayo 14. Edom punorachomonio.

Say the pranam mantra with hands joined and ring the ghanta.

<u>Ganapati:</u>

Dhyan: *Aum kharbang sthula tanung gajendra badanang lambodarang sundaram prasyanda gandha lubbdha madhupa byallola gandasthalam| Dantaghata vidari tari rudhiroi sinduro shovakarang vande shaila suta sutang Ganapating siddhi pradang kamadang||*

Call Riddhi siddhi luv subh sahit Ganapati dev with avahan aadi pancha mudra. Do panch/dash upachar puja.

Pranam mantra: *Aum vakratunda mahakaya surya koti samaprabha nirvighnyam Kurume deva sarva kaarye su sarvadam| Ekadanta mahakya lambodara gajananam bighno naasho karang debong herombong pranamammoham||*

Surya:

Dhyan: *Aum raktambuj asan mashesh gunaik sindhung bhanung samastha jagata dheepam bhajami| Padmadyang bhaybaran dadhatang korabjoi mraniko moulim ruran angaruching trinetram||*

Call sahparivar Surya dev with avahan aadi pancha mudra. Do panch/dash upachar puja.

Pranam mantra: *Aum japakusuma sankhasang kashyapiyang mahadhutim dwantarim sarva paapaghnyam pranohtashmin divakaram|*

Vishnu:

Dhyan: *Aum dhayet sada savitri mandala madhyabarti Narayana sarashijashana sannibeshtang| Keyubaranang kanak kundalabaan kiritihaari hironmoy bapudhrita sankha chakram||*

Call soh parivar laxmi sahit Vishnu dev with avahan aadi pancha mudra. Do panch/dash upachar puja.

Pranam mantra: *Aum brahmanya devaya gobrahmanya hitayacho jagadhitaya Shri Krishnaya govindaya nama namaha| Heh Krishna karuna sindhu deena bandhu jagatpataye gopesha gopikakanta radhakanta namastute||*

Shiv:

Dhyan: *Aum dhyaynityang maheshang rajatagiri nibhang charuchandra batangsang ratno kalpo jwalasang*

*parashu mriga barabhiti hastang prasannanam|
Padmasinhang samantat stuto mamaro ganoi bhyagro
kirting basanang biswadyang biswa beejang nikhila
bhaya haarang pancha vakram trinetram||*

Call Soh parivar Parvati sahit Shiva with avahan aadi
pancha mudra. Do panch/dash upachar puja.

Pranam mantra: *Aum namah Shivaya shantaya
karonatrayo hetobe nivedayami chatmang twang gatim
parameshwara|*

Jai Durga:

Dhyan: *Aum kalabhravang katakhoiribi kulang
bhayadang mouli bardhendu rekhang shankhang
chakrang kripanang trishikhamapi karoi ruddhabha
hantim trinetram| Singha skandha dhi rurang
tribhubanam akhilam tejasha purayantim, dhyayed
durgang jayakhyang tridesh paribritang sebitang
siddhikamoi||*

Call soh parivar Jai Durga devi with avahan aadi pancha
mudra. Do panch/dash upachar puja.

Pranam mantra: *Aum sarva mangalya mangalye shive
sarbartho shadhike sharanye trambake gauri Narayani
namastute| Sishti stithi vinashanang shaktibhute sanatani
gunashraye gunamaye Narayani namastute||
Sharanagata dheenartha paritrayana parayane sarva
syarthe hare Durge Narayani namastute| Aum Jai
Durgaoi namaha Aum Katayayani namaha Aum
Mahishasur mardinibhyo namaha||*

Other important pujas

Navagraha Puja:

Ete gandhapushpe Rabigrahay namaha, Ete gandhapushpe Somay namaha, Ete gandhapushpe Mangalaye namaha, Ete gandhapushpe Budhay namaha, Ete gandhapushpe Brihaspataya namaha, Ete gandhapushpe Sukrayo namaha, Ete gandhapushpe Sanishchayayo namaha, Ete gandhapushpe Rahube namaha, Ete gandhapushpe Ketubhyo grohabye namaha|

Dikpal Puja:

Ete gandhapushpe Indraya namaha, Ete gandhapushpe Aganaye namaha, Ete gandhapushpe Yamaye namaha, Ete gandhapushpe Nairutyaya namaha, Ete gandhapushpe Varunaya namaha, Ete gandhapushpe Vayube namaha, Ete gandhapushpe Kuberaya namaha, Ete gandhapushpe Eeshanay namaha, Ete gandhapushpe Brahmanyaye namaha, Ete gandhapushpe Anantaya namaha|

Dash Avatar Puja:

Ete gandhapushpe Matsya avatarya namaha, Ete gandhapushpe Kurmo avatarya namaha, Ete gandhapushpe Varaha avatarya namaha, Ete gandhapushpe Narsingh avatarya namaha, Ete gandhapushpe Vamana avatarya namaha, Ete gandhapushpe Parashurama avatarya namaha, Ete gandhapushpe Ram avatarya namaha, Ete gandhapushpe Balaram avatarya namaha, Ete gandhapushpe Krishna avatarya namaha, Ete gandhapushpe Buddha avatarya namaha, Ete gandhapushpe Kalki avatarya namaha|

Dash-mahavidya puja:
Ete gandhapushpe Kalikaoi namaha, Ete gandhapushpe Taraoi namaha, Ete gandhapushpe Tripurasundaribhyo namaha, Ete gandhapushpe Bhubaneshwaryai namaha, Ete gandhapushpe Bhairavioi namaha, Ete gandhapushpe Chinnamastaoi avatarya namaha, Ete gandhapushpe Dhumavattoi namaha, Ete gandhapushpe Bagalaoi namaha, Ete gandhapushpe Matangibhyo namaha, Ete gandhapushpe Kamalatmikaoi namaha|

Shodosh upachar puja of Saraswati

Pranayam: With *"Aum Saraswattai namaha"* mantra for 7 times.

Tarpan: Hold some rice, chandan and siddhi between ring finger and thumb in tatwa-mudra on a copper patra and pour water on it with mantra for 7 times: *Aum Saraswati tarpayami swaha|*

Dhyan: Chant the dhyan mantra of Saraswati in kurma mudra with flower, bilwapatra in hand. After dhyan, give flowers to her feet.

Archana patra: Clean a good looking plate and use it to keep everything for archana (by sprinkling water with tripatrika with archana mantra and puja with gandha-pusha) to Saraswati before its utsarga. Clean your hands after every archana. **Chant the specific Gayatri after every Utsarga mantra.**

1. **Rajat asanaya: Archana mantra:** *Bong etoshmoing Rajat asanaya namah| Ete gandhapushpe Rajat asanaya*

namah| Etot adhipataye devaya Shri Vishnavay namah| Sampradanaya Rajat asanaya Aum Saraswattai namah||

Utsarga mantra: *Aum asanang grihu devim yat kritang sobhonang moya sarbo kaamo falang dehi Aum Saraswattai namah| Edang Rajat asanaya Aum Saraswattai namah||*

2. **Swagatang:** *Aum yatshodarshang michonti deva shobistho siddhoye tasmain te param aisharyo sagatam suswasgatam swagatan chame| Aum kritartho honu grihata hasmin safala jibono momoh, Agoto debo debeshe sushwagatang medong bopu| Aum bhur bhubha swaha Swarna Saraswati swa paribarahoi swabahonaoi swa gonaoi swagatang sushwagatang kushalang kuru||*
Pranam: *Aum swagatanu grihatahasmin suswagata midang subham, prasanna bhawa devesi kripan kuru haripriye|*

3. **Paadya/water to clean legs: Archana mantra:** *Bong etoshmoing paadyang namah| Ete gandhapushpe paadyang namah| Etot adhipataye devaya Shri Vishnavay namah| Sampradanaya paadyang Aum Saraswattai namah||*

Utsarga mantra: *Aum padyang grihinu devata sarbadukkhang paharakam kriyoshyo barade deva namaste vishnuballabhe| Etong Paadyang Aum Saraswattai namah||*

4. **Vishesh-Arghya: Archana mantra:** *Bong etoshmoing Arghaya namah| Ete gandhapushpe Arghaya namah| Etot adhipataye devaya Shri Vishnavay namah| Sampradanaya Arghaya Aum Saraswattai namah||*

Utsarga mantra: *Aum durba akshata samyuktam gandha pushpo tatha param shobhenang sankha patrasthang grihinang Aum Saraswattai namah| Esho arghaya Aum Saraswattai namah||*

5. **Achomonio/water to clean mouth: Archana mantra:** *Bong etoshmoing achomonio namah| Ete gandhapushpe achomonio namah| Etot adhipataye devaya Shri Vishnavay namah| Sampradanaya Achomonio Aum Saraswattai namah||*

Utsarga mantra: *Aum mandakinastu jat baari sarba paapa harang subham grihanang achomonio twam moya bhakta nibeditam| Edam Achomonio Aum Saraswattai namah||*

6. **Madhuparkayo/patra with honey: Archana mantra:** *Bong etoshmoing Madhuparkayo namah| Ete gandhapushpe Madhuparkayo namah| Etot adhipataye devaya Shri Vishnavay namah| Sampradanaya Madhuparkayo Aum Saraswattai namah||*

Utsarga mantra: *Aum madhuparkam maha devim pari-kalpitam moya nibeditam bhakta grihu Saraswattai| Esho Madhuparkayo Aum Saraswattai namah||*

7. **Punorachomonio/water to clean mouth: Archana mantra:** *Bong etoshmoing punorachomonio namah| Ete gandhapushpe punorachomonio namah| Etot adhipataye devaya Shri Vishnavay namah| Sampradanaya punorachomonio Aum Saraswattai namah||*

Utsarga mantra: *Edam punorachomonio Aum Saraswattai namah||*

8. Snanio/ water for bathing: Archana mantra: *Bong etoshmoing snanio namah| Ete gandhapushpe snanio namah| Etot adhipataye devaya Shri Vishnavay namah| Sampradanaya snanio Aum Saraswattai namah||*

Utsarga mantra: *Aum jalancha sheetalang swacchang suddha hasto manoharang snanarthe pracchayami Saraswating| Etot Snanio jalang Aum Saraswattai namah||*

9. Bastra/cloth: Archana mantra: *Bong etoshmoing bastraya namah| Ete gandhapushpe bastraya namah| Etot adhipataye devaya Shri Vishnavay namah| Sampradanaya bastraya Aum Saraswattai namah||*

Utsarga mantra: *Aum subukhlam paramang devam nutanang su monoharang, moya nibeditam bhakta bastra te progrihitong Saraswating| Edam bastra Aum Saraswattai namah||*

10. Abhoran/jwellery: Archana mantra: *Bong etoshmoing Swarna/Rajat abhoranayo namah| Ete gandhapushpe Swarna/Rajat abhoranayo namah| Etot adhipataye devaya Shri Vishnavay namah| Sampradanaya Swarna/Rajat abhoranayo Aum Saraswattai namah||*

Utsarga mantra: *Aum divya ratno samyuktam bahi banu samoprabha kartani shovoy eshanti alankara Saraswatiwar| Moya alankara krito dev anga lagna monoharana, moya nibeditam bhaktam alankara progrihottam| Edam Swarna/Rajat Abhoranayo Aum Saraswattai namah||*

11. Gandho/chandan/scent: Archana mantra: *Bong etoshmoing Gandhaya namah| Ete gandhapushpe Gandhaya namah| Etot adhipataye devaya Shri Vishnavay namah| Sampradanaya Gandhaya Aum Saraswattai namah||*

Utsarga mantra: *Aum sharirang te nah janami chastang noibocho-noibocho moya niveditam gandhanang prati grihjjang bilwapattam| Esho Gandhaya Aum Saraswattai namah||*

12. Pushpa/flower: Archana mantra: *Bong etoshmoing Pushpang namah| Ete gandhapushpe Pushpang namah| Etot adhipataye devaya Shri Vishnavay namah| Sampradanaya Pushpang Aum Saraswattai namah||*

Utsarga mantra: *Aum pushpong manoharang romang sugandhi devang nirmittong hridyang adwitamam arghyang devo sattang prati grihajjotam| Etong Pushpang Aum Saraswattai namah||*

13. Garland/mala: Archana mantra: *Bong etoshmoing pushpomallong namah| Ete gandhapushpe pushpomallong namah| Etot adhipataye devaya Shri Vishnavay namah| Sampradanaya pushpomallong Aum Saraswattai namah||*

Utsarga mantra: *Aum sutreno gritthitang mallong nana pushpong samanwitam sriyukto lombo malancho grihanang Saraswating| Etong pushpomallong Aum Saraswattai namah||*

14. Dhup/incense stick: Archana mantra: *Bong etoshmoing dhupaya namah| Ete gandhapushpe dhupaya* *namah| Etot adhipataye devaya Shri Vishnavay namah| Sampradanaya dhupaya Aum Saraswattai namah||*

Utsarga mantra: *Aum banaspati raso devya gandhohang su monoharang moya niveditang bhakta dhupayay prati grihajjang| Esho Dhupaya Aum Saraswattai namah||*

Chant specific gayatri. Arati with it with ghanta sound 10 times around umbilicus and keep it at Saraswati's left side.

15. **Deep: Archana mantra:** *Bong etoshmoing deepang namah| Ete gandhapushpe deepang namah| Etot adhipataye devaya Shri Vishnavay namah| Sampradanaya deepang Aum Saraswattai namah||*

Utsarga mantra: *Aum agni jyoting rabi jyotish chandra jyoti swa chaiba cha jyotisyang uttama devo deepayang prati grihajjang| Esho Deepang Aum Saraswattai namah||*

Chant specific gayatri. Arati with it with ghanta sound and keep it on Saraswati's right side.

16. **Naivedya: Archana mantra:** *Bong etoshmoing khando fal mul aadi sahit sopokaran naivedyang namah| Ete gandhapushpe naivedyang namah| Etot adhipataye devaya Shri Vishnavay namah| Nivedayami naivedyang Aum Saraswattai namah||*

Utsarga mantra: Water spread around food: *Fatt* mantra|

Show thumb: *Shri Vishnu pundarikashyo punarthu|*

Utsarga: With water in right hand: *Aum Etot amrita patranamasi swaha| Etot naivedyang Aum Saraswattai namah||*

Chant specific gayatri.

17. **Panarthodokayo/ drinking water: Archana mantra:** *Bong etoshmoing Panarthodokayo namah| Ete gandhapushpe Panarthodokayo namah| Etot adhipataye devaya Shri Vishnavay namah| Sampradanaya Panarthodokayo Aum Saraswattai namah||*

Utsarga mantra: *Aum panartho shashilang debong karpoor aadi suvashitam sarvatripti karang swacchang apoyami namastute| Aum jwalancha shitalang swaccham sugandhi paripooritam moya niveditam bhaktam paanartho prati grihajjang| Edang Panarthodokayo Aum Saraswattai namah||*

18. **Mishtanna/ sweets: Archana mantra:** *Bong etoshmoing mishtannabhyang namah| Ete gandhapushpe mishtannabhyang namah| Etot adhipataye devaya Shri Vishnavay namah| Sampradanaya mishtannabhyang Aum Saraswattai namah||*

Utsarga mantra: Modak: *Aum modakam madhu sanjukta sarkaraadi bihimishritong sursung madhuro majja Saraswating twang pari grihajjatang| Etot mishtannabhyang Aum Saraswattai namah||*
Laddoo: *Aum laddookang param swadhang nana roop bivinitang su mishting shobhenong devong tat etot prati grihajjatang| Etot mishtannabhyang Aum Saraswattai namah||*

19. **Punorachomonio: Archana mantra:** *Bong etoshmoing punorachomonio namah| Ete gandhapushpe punorachomonio namah| Etot adhipataye devaya Shri Vishnavay namah| Sampradanaya punorachomonio Aum Saraswattai namah||*

Utsarga mantra: *Edam punorachomonio Aum Saraswattai namah||*

20. **Tambul/paan: Archana mantra:** *Bong etoshmoing tambulang namah| Ete gandhapushpe tambulang namah| Etot adhipataye devaya Shri Vishnavay namah| Sampradanaya tambulang Aum Saraswattai namah||*

Utsarga mantra: *Aum falapatram samyuktam karpoorena subhasitam moya nibeditam bhakta tambulang pratigrijjhotang| Etong Tambulang Aum Saraswattai namah||*

21. **Narikilo dakayo/coconut water: Archana mantra:** *Bong etoshmoing Narikilo Dokayo namah| Ete gandhapushpe Narikilo dakayo namah| Etot adhipataye devaya Shri Vishnavay namah| Sampradanaya Narikilo dakayo Aum Saraswattai namah||*

Utsarga mantra: *Aum paanartho pranarthoncho sukharthoncho briksha aagre amritadwyam sarbasatto su karma narikila grihanang me| Etong Narikilo dakayo Aum Saraswattai namah||*

22. **Durba: Archana mantra:** *Bong etoshmoing Durbang namah| Ete gandhapushpe Durbang namah| Etot adhipataye devaya Shri Vishnavay namah| Sampradanaya Durbang Aum Saraswattai namah||*

Utsarga mantra: *Aum namaste swarge deva namaste mukha mokhadye durba grihan devo tang mang nistaraye sarvatah| Etang Durbang Aum Saraswattai namah||*

23. **Chaand mala: Archana mantra:** *Bong etoshmoing chaand mallong namah| Ete gandhapushpe chaand mallong namah| Etot adhipataye devaya Shri Vishnavay namah| Sampradanaya chaand mallong Aum Saraswattai namah||*

Utsarga: *Esho Chaand mallong Aum Saraswattai namah||*

24. **Sindoor: Archana mantra:** *Bong etoshmoing Sindoorang namah| Ete gandhapushpe Sindoorang namah| Etot adhipataye devaya Shri Vishnavay namah| Sampradanaya Sindoorang Aum Saraswattai namah||*

Utsarga mantra: *Aum sinduribo pradbone sughnonasho bathpromi yaha patyanti yabaha ghritashya dhara ashruho nah baji kashtaha bhindonong nurmibhiha pinbomanaha| Etong Sindoorang Aum Saraswattai namah||*

Paath the **pranam mantra** with ghanta: *Aum jaya jaya devi chara chara shaare kucho jugo shobhito mukta haare bina pustaka ranjita haste bhagawati bharati devi namastute||*

Bhog nivedan

Archana mantra: *Bong etoshmoing byanjan aadi sahit sopokaran <Khrisharannam(Pulao), Luchinam (Puri), Ghritobhokkhannam (Khichdi), Shiddhoannang (White*

rice), *or Paramannang* (Payesham)> *Naivedyang namah|
Ete gandhapushpe <Khrisharannam, Luchinam,
Ghritobhokkhannam, Shiddhoannang, or Paramannang>
Naivedyang namah| Etot adhipataye devaya Shri
Vishnavay namah| Sampradanaya <Khrisharannam,
Luchinam, Ghritobhokkhannam, Shiddhoannang,
Paramannang> Naivedyang Aum Saraswattai namah||*

Utsarga mantra: Water spread around food: *Fatt* mantra|
Show thumb: *Shri vishnu pundarikashyo punarthu|*
Left index from left to right: *Hng* mantra|
Dhenu mudra: *Bng* mantra
Matsya mudra pradarshan, *"Aum Saraswattai namaha"*
jaap (minimum 10 times)
With water in right hand: *Aum Etot amritopatranamasi
swaha|*

*Etot <Khrisharannam, Luchinam, Ghritobhokkhannam,
Shiddhoannang, Paramannang> Naivedyang Aum
Saraswattai nivedayami||*

Hamsha vahan puja:
Do the pran pratishta of hamsha vahan in the same way as
Maa Saraswati and call them with aavahan aadi panch
mudras.

Dhyan mantra: Om hang satyam atma rupashi
dwinetram tikshno jyoti samanwitam baarina
madhyastham sarva diko chalanwitam|
Do puja with panch upachar with: *Aum Hamshaya
namaha|*

Pranam mantra: Oum Sarva shakti samanwitam brahma
gyanam virajitam sarba barna shobhitam baag devi
vahanam pranamyaham||

Give water to the ghat three times with this mantra:
Aum bhadrakalloi namo nityang Saraswattai namo namaha, Veda vedanga vedanta vidyasthanebhya evacha swaha|

Saraswati parivar puja:
*Ete gandhapushpe **Laxmi** devi namaha, Ete gandhapushpe **Shivaoi** namaha, Ete gandhapushpe **Durgaoi** namaha, Ete gandhapushpe **Karthikai** namaha, Ete gandhapushpe **Brahmaoi** namaha, Ete gandhapushpe **Gayatri** devyai namaha, Ete gandhapushpe **Savitri** devyai namaha, Ete gandhapushpe **vadyayantraoi** namaha, Ete gandhapushpe **kamalaoi** namaha, Ete gandhapushpe **lekhanibhyo** namaha, Ete gandhapushpe **mashyadharebhyo** namaha, Ete gandhapushpe **pustakebhyo** namaha, Ete gandhapushpe **shrubay** namaha|*

Saraswati stotra

Read the stotra in pranam mudra:

Sweto padmasana devi sweto pushpo sushobita, swetambaradhara devi, nitya sweto-gandhanu lepanah, swetaksutra hastacha, sweto chandana charchita, sweto veena dhara subhra, swetalankaro bhushita| Vandita siddha gandharvairchita suradanavai pujita munibhi sarvei rishibhi stutaye sada||
Stotrena aneno twang devim jagatdhatrim Saraswatim| Ye smarantim trisandhyam sarve vidyam lavantute| Eti Shri Shri Padmapurane Saraswati stotram sampurnam||

SARASWATI VIDMAHE

Prarthana mantra:

Ya kundendu tushaara haara dhavala, ya swetapadmasana, ya veenadhara dandamandita bhuja, yaa Brahmachuto shankara pravitibhir devoi sada vandita| Saa mang paatu Saraswati bhagawati nihshesh jaddhapaha||
Aum yatha na devo bhagawan brahmaloko pitamaha twam paritajya shantisthyet taha bhawa barapradam| Aum vedah shastrah sarvani nrittyo geeta dikanchayet, naa bihinang twaya tatha me shantu siddhayah||
Laxmir medha dhara pushti gauri tushtir prabha dhritih| Etabhi pahi tanur bhir ashtabhirmanang Saraswattai namo namaha||

Arati

Do arati with panch pradeep, karpoor, dhup, vishesh arghya, hand fan, vastra and flowers. Side by side in the left hand play the ghanta and other instruments and songs may also be played according to family traditions. One of the song is as follows:

Om jai Saraswati mata, Maiya jai Saraswati mata Sadhgun bayebhaw Shalini, Tribhuan bikkhyata, Om Jai Saraswati mata|
Chandrawaadini padamaasini, Dhuti mangal karee Sohe Shubh hans sawaari, Atul tej dhaaree, Om Jai Saraswati mata|
Baayen kar me Veena, daayen kar mala Shish mukut mandti sohe, Gal motian mala, Om Jai Saraswati mata|
Devi sharan jo aaye, unka udhaar kiya Paithee manthra daasi, Rawan sanhaar kiya, Om Jai Saraswati mata|
Vidya gyan pradayeni, Gyan prakash bharo Moh gyan ki birtha, Jag se maat haro, Om Jai Saraswati mata|

Dhoop deep phal mewa, Maa sweekaar karo Gyan chachoo de mata, Jag nisaar karo, Om Jai Saraswati mata|
Maa Saraswati Ji ki arti, Jo koi jan gaawe Hitkaaree sukhkaaree, Gyan Bhakti paawe, Om Jai Saraswati mata|

Pushpanjali

One sole pushpanjali has to be done by the priest. Then he/she shall make others do the pushpanjali. Pushpanjali is done with 3 mantras. Make the devotees wash their hands with clean water and do achaman. Ask them to chant in namaskar mudra:

Aum Vishnu Aum Vishnu Aum Vishnu|
Aum tat Vishnu paramam padam sada pashyanti Suraya dibibo Chakshuratatam|
Namah Vishnu Namah Vishnu Namah Vishnu||
Aum Apavitra pavitrava sarvavastang gato pibah yatsmare pundorikakshyang shabajhyabhyang abhyantaro suchi| Namah Suchi Namah Suchi Namah Suchi ||

Give gandha-pushpa and bilwa-patra in their hands and ask them to say these three mantras:

1. *Aum Saraswati mahabhaage vidye kamala lochane viswa roope vishal-akshi vidyang devi namastute| Etot sachandana bilwapatrasahit gandhapushpa pushpanjali Aum Laxmi Narayan sahitaoi Saraswati devi bho namaha||*
2. *Aum bhadrakalloi namo nityang Saraswattai namo namaha, Veda vedanga vedanta vidyasthanebhya evacha| Etot sachandana gandhapushpa pushpanjali Aum Riddhi siddhi Vinayak Luv subh sahit Saraswati devi bho namaha|*

3. *Aum jaya jaya devi chara chara shaare kucho jugo shobito mukta haare veena pustaka ranjita haste bhagawati bharati devi namastute| Etot sachandana gandhapushpa pushpanjali Aum sarva dev devi swaroopinyai laxmi narayan sahitaoi Saraswati devi bho namaha|*

Tell the devotees to offer the flowers to Saraswati. Throwing flowers may lead to falling of those on the ground so tell them to collect the pushpa in a patra and then the priest must offer it to Saraswati. Now tell them to namaskar Saraswati:

Pranam: *Aum yatha na devo bhagawan brahmaloko pitamaha twam paritajya shantisthyet taha bhawa barapradam| Aum vedah shastrah sarvani nrittyo geeta dikanchayet, naa bihinang twaya tatha me shantu siddhayah||*
Laxmir medha dhara pushti gauri tushtir prabha dhritih| Etabhi pahi tanur bhir ashtabhirmanang Saraswattai namo namaha||

Shantir jal:
Sprinkle water from the Bishesh arghya/saman arghya with this mantra:

Aum richong bachong prapadye manur yong prapadye, sambatsyare byatite tu, bara-dam bara-bhawah-ha|
Aum Swastino Indra briddhaswaha, Swastino pushpa biswavedaha, Swastino sakshat aristonemi swastino Brihaspati dadhatu|
Aum Swasti Aum Swasti Aum Swasti||

Starting of study, puja mantra for children:

Oum panchabyam pujayem laxmim pushpo dhupo deepo anno baari bhi mashyadhara lekhanincha likhet maaghe mashe shuklepakshe panchami yah shriyah| Tasya purbanno ebeho karyo saraswattai utsabaha||

Shri Shri Saraswati Puja Yajna Vidhi

Yajna is a huge term, it includes puja and burning of the sacrificial fire for a great cause for several days and nights. The short process of Yajna which can be done in Kali yuga to achieve the same benefits of Yajna is known as the homa/home/hawan.

These things required for homa:
Yajna kund, kush asan, deep, dhup, **kush**: Asan for pranita and prokshani patra and brahma, 2 for pavitra, 3 for pavitra chedan, 3 samarjaka and upajaman kush, **Spruk, Shrub, prokshani, pranita patra**, **knife** to cut kush, **kosha-kushi, kamandulu, wood, pat-kathi, karpoor, chandan, pushpa, rice, black til, fruit, arya-patra with ghee.**
All these things are to be arranged in this fashion:

Arrangement for Yajna/Homa

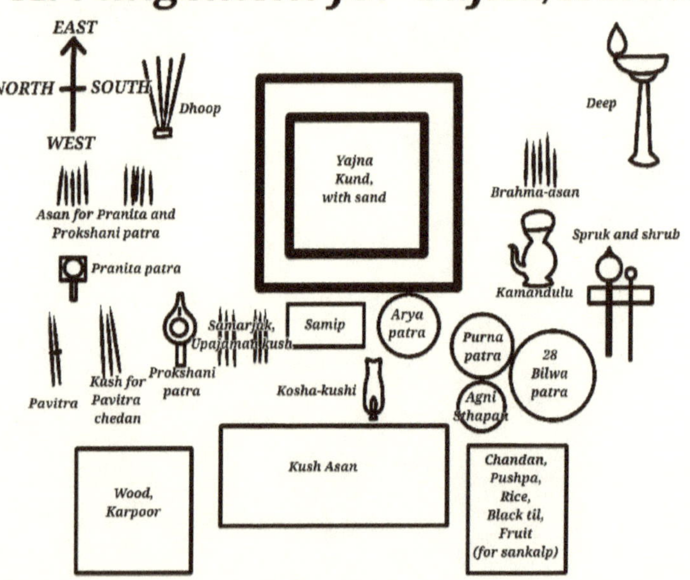

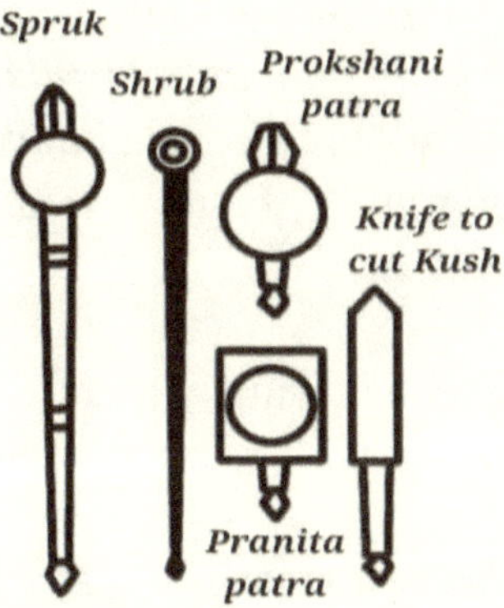

Fig. Wooden items required for Yajna

Now, as you have collected all the required materials, you can start the homa:

Achaman and Vishnu Smaran

You have to follow the same process of achaman. Do the achaman for three times. And then do the Vishnu smaran as it is in puja.

Swastivachan

Fill kushi with rice, close it and chant:

Aum kartabhehasmin subha Shri Shri Saraswati home karmani Aum purnahang bhavantu bhrubantu Aum purnahang bhavantu bhrubantu Aum purnahang bhavantu bhrubantu|
Aum Purnahang Aum Purnahang Aum Purnahang||
Aum kartabhehasmin Subha Shri Shri Saraswati home karmani Aum Swasti bhavantu bhrubantu Aum Swasti bhavantu bhrubantu Aum Swasti bhavantu bhrubantu|

Aum Swasti Aum Swasti Aum Swasti||
Aum kartabhehasmin Subha Shri Shri Saraswati home karmani Aum Hriddhi bhavantu bhrubantu Aum Hriddhi bhavantu bhrubantu Aum Hriddhi bhavantu bhrubantu|
Aum Hriddhyatam Aum Hriddhyatam Aum Hriddhyatam||

Spread rice along with playing ghanta:
Swastino Indra briddhaswaha, Swastino pushpa biswavedaha,
Swastino sakshat aristonemi swastino Brihaspati dadhatu|
Aum Swasti Aum Swasti Aum Swasti||

Swasti sukta:
Put kushi in front and with ghanta:

Aum Gananang twa ganapatevyo hawamahe,
Aum Priyanang twa priyapatebhyo hawamahe,
Aum Nidhinang twa nidhinapatebhyo hawa mahe baso mamaha||
Aum Swasti Aum Swasti Aum Swasti||

Gayatri paath

This is very important for Yajna. You will have to chant the Gayatri mantra at least 10 times and **cover your head** with a cloth so that none of your hair falls into the Agni.

Sankalpa

In Kosha-kushi or panchpatra keep panch-shashya, rice, any fruit (except betel nut), flower etc. and sit facing north with right knee touching the ground and left above (with your holy thread in hand- if you have one), touch the fruit and say the **sankalpa vakya:**

Aum Vishnurang tatsad adyo <month, tithi according to Saka calendar> <Pujaris' names with gotra> (karoyet <beneficiary name with gotra> mot sankalpito) Shri shri Saraswati priti kaamo homa karmahang <korishyami- for others/korishye- for yourself>|

Sankapla sukta: Provide the fruit to the Saraswati and say:

Aum yajjagrata durmoiti devim tathoubouti tathouboshyo durgama jyotishyang jyoti rekhang tanme mann Shiva sankalpa matsyu| Aum aayam arombhyo subharombhyo asya sankalpito rasya asya siddhi dhaarastu||

Gandha dravya archana

Sprinkle water on flowers and chandan and say:

Bong etoshmoing gandha dravyay namah| Ete gandhapushpe gandha dravyay namah| Etot adhipataye devaya Shri Brahma Vishnu Maheshwaray namah| Sampradanaya gandha dravya Aum Agnaye namah||

Saman argha sthapan

Same procedure as in puja part.

Pushpa suddhi

Flowers must be mixed with Chandan. Touch Pushpa and say:

Aum Pushpe Pushpe maha pushpe shu pushpe pushpa shambhabe, Pushpachaya bakirnecho hong fatt swaha|

Spread samanargha jal on pushpa and chant:

Pushpaketu Raja hasthe sattyo sammukho somoddhyayo hong|

Asan Suddhi

Same process as in Puja.

Utkara-nirashon

Cover the yajna pund with clean sand, put 3 pradesh-praman sized kush with their tips towards east and pick up small amount of sand from the west side of the kush in your hand with tatwa mudra and throw the sand towards Eeshan (North-East) direction.

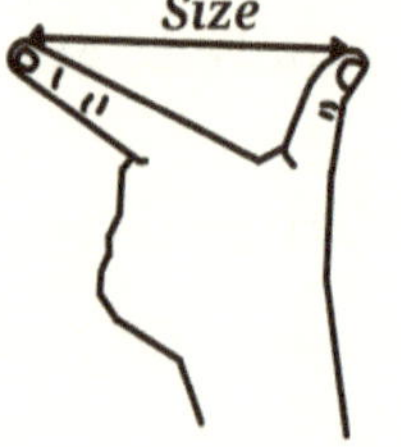

Place the wood and karpoor on the sand as you like such that the wood catches fire as soon as you touch them with fire.

Agni-sthapana

In a small patra, take two pieces of karpoor and light them with fire. Throw one piece of karpoor with fire towards South-west direction. And say:

Aum krabyadhdam Agnim prohinome durang Yama rajam gacchatu riprobaha|

Take the other karpoor and drop it in the yajna kunda so as the woods catches the fire:

Om ehoibaya mitaro jatobedaha debebya habyang bahatu prajanana|

Kritanta/Pranam

Namaskar mudra: *Aum sarbatoha panipadantaha sarvatokshe shiromukhaha viswa rupo mahanagni pranetoha sarva karmashu|*

Brahma-sthapana

On the South of Yajna kunda place some kush on the ground and place a kamandulu/umbrella/Narayan on it. And consider that to be the Brahma/knowledgeble person who will guide your Yajna:

Namaskar: *Aum ahe daidhi shavyo datsa tishtanyasha sadane shid jyoasmad paata karaha|*

Give garland and pushpa to Brahma. Sprinkle water from samanarghya to brahma: *Aum Sidami|*

Take one kush from the asan of Brahma and throw it towards the south west direction and say:

Aum nairutosto papanashaya teno bayam dwishmo|

Make Brahma face the agni of yajna kund and say:

Aum edamahang brihaspate sadne sidami prasuto debena sobitra tadagnye probrobimi tadbyabe debeno twat prithibing|

Pranita-patra sthapana

Place the Pranita patra in the north side of Agni and clean it with samanarghya water and put some
water into it.

Kush astaran

Surround the Yajna kund with 3 kush on each side in clock-wise direction. The tips of the kush have to face east-wards.

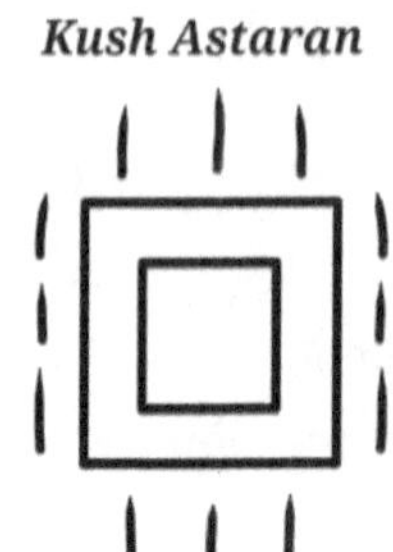

Pavitra-chedan

Tie two kush together and tear the two kush with three kush together in pradesh size. Say: *Aum pavitrashou Vaishnavou|*
Sprinkle water on it: *Aum Vishnur manasha putesthaha|*

Place the pavitra on prokshani patra horizontally then put it on the pronita patra horizontally and then transfer water from pronita patra to the prokshani patra with pavitra for three times.

Lift the prokshani patra with your right hand, transfer to left hand, drop some water onto the ground and keep it back in its place.
Sprinkle water from pranita patra with pavitra on Shrub, Spruk, Arya patra, Purna patra, and then keep the pavitra back on pranita patra horizontally.

Arya-sanskar

Arya in Sanskrit means ghee. Melt the ghee by keeping the arya patra besides the Agni. Pick up a burning wood and turn it three times around the arya patra and keep it back into the kund.

Take the arya patra upon the Agni, heat it and rub its lower side with Pavitra kush. Repeat it three times.
Keep the patra in the north of Agni, then move it clockwise towards west of Agni.

Take the pavitra kush with ankush mudra on both the hands and clean any debris on the ghee. Lift some ghee with the middle part of the pavitra kush and give it to Agni with this mantra:
Aum savitushwa prasava uth punnama chhidreno pavitreno vasoha Suryashcha rishmibhiha swaha|

Keep the pavitra back in prokshani patra.

Shrub, spruk sanskar

Rub some ghee on the shrub and spruk and face it downwards (Adham-mukha) on the agni, heat it, rub with Samarjan kush and water on both sides and repeat for three times.
Give the samarjan kush into Agni.
Take the three Upajamana kush with right hand, transfer to left hand and keep it over the heart. Take the 3 Samip with right han, mix with ghee and give it to Agni without any mantra.

Agni-paryukshan

Do a pradaksina of Agni from its eeshan (North east) direction clockwise and back along with spreading water from the prokshani patra with the pavitra kush with this mantra:

Aum esho devaha pradishonu sarbaha purbo ha onso jataha sa uh garbhentaha esaha jataha sha janishya manaha pratyang janastishtoti sarbato mukhaha

Sit on your asan again. Now onwards the pranita patra will be termed as patrantar.
This is the end of Kushondika.

First ahuti

With Shrub give the ghee to Agni in the specific directions and the remaining ghee is shed on to the patrantar with *"edam"* mantra:
Eastward on north side: *Aum Prajapataye swaha edam Prajapataye*
Eastward on south side: *Aum Indraya swaha Edam Indraya*
North-east: *Aum Agnaye swaha Edam Agnaye*
South-west: *Aum Shomayo swaha Edam Shomaye*

Keep the shrub back again with Adham mukha.

Homa sankalpa

Take the sankalpa facing towards east and with the 28 ghee mixed bilwa patra in hand:

Vishnurong tat sat adyo <month, paksha and tithi> tirthou Shri <pujari name> <Gotra> gotrashya karoyet Saraswati priti kaam arthe Shri Shri Saraswati puja home karmane "Aum pada pada baag vaadini devi Saraswattai swaha" eti mantrena pratikena pathena astha binshaka sajjya bilwa patra homahang <korishyami/korishye>|

Om yajjagrata durmoiti debong tothouboti tothoubotsyo durgomo to jyotishyang jyotirekhong tanme mann Shiva sankalpamatsyu|

Add black sesame seeds to the ghee. Mix a Samip with ghee and give it to Agni.

Mahavyariti Yajna

With shrub give ghee to Agni with these mantras and shed the remaining ghee on to the patrantar with "*edam*" mantra:

Aum Prajapati rishi gayatri chandau Agni devata mahavyariti home ey viniyogaha:
Aum bhu swaha, edam bhu x3

Aum Prajapati rishi ushnik chandau Vayu devata maha byariti home ey viniyogaha:
Aum bhubha swaha edam swaha x3

Aum Prajapati rishi anushtup chandaha Surya devata maha vyariti home ey viniyogaha:
Aum swa swana edam swa ×3

Aum Prajapati rishi brihati chandou Prajapati devata vyasta samastha maha byarit homey viniyogha:
Aum Bhu bhuva Swa swaha Edam Bhubhuva Swa swaha

Saraswati homa

Say: *Om Agne twam baladh namasi*

Dhyan: *Aum Pringa bhushma shruke shakshoha pinanga jatharo runaha| Chagastha saksho sutrognini saptarchi shakti dharakaha||*

Avahan with avahan aadi panch mudra: Om Baladh agnei eha gaccha eha gaccho....

Do a **panch upachar** puja of Baladh agni with gandha, pushpa, dhup, deep and ghee.

Utsarga of 28 bilwa patra:

Sprinkle saman arghya water: *Bong etebhyo sajjyo bilwa patrebhyo namaha×3*
Gandha pushpa: *Ete gandha pushpe om sajjyo bilwa pabrebhyo namaha| Etot adhipate devaya Brahma Vishnu Maheshwaray namaha|*
Aum sampradanebhyo bilwapatre Aum Saraswattai namaha||

Give the bilwa patra one by one into the Agni after again mixing them with ghee with the mantra: *"Aum pada pada baag vaadini devi Saraswattai swaha"* directly into the fire.
Again do a **Mahavyariti yajna**.

Prayaschitya homa

Yajna is a large process, making mistakes here is easy. So one should do a prayaschitya homa to please agni:

Sankhipta Mahavayariti homa:

Aum bhu swaha edam bhu
Aum bhuba swaha edam bhuba
Aum swa swaha edam swa
Aum bhur bhuba swa swaha edam bhur bhuba swa|

Sankalpa: Just like normal sankalpa taken:

Vishnurong tat sat adyo <month, paksha and tithi> tirthou Shri <name> <gotra> Shri Saraswati priti hasmin home karmani yadoi-gunang jatang tad dosh proshmanay tanno agne ettadivhi panchavi manraye payaschitto homahang karishyami/korishye||

Aum yajjagrata durmoiti debong tothouboti tothoubotsyo durgomo to jyohishyang jyotirekhong tanme manah Shiva sankalpamatsyu|

Aum Agne twam vidhu namasi

Dhyan: *Aum Pringa bhushma shruke shakshoha pinanga jatharo runaha| Chagastha saksho sutrognini saptarchi shakti dharakaha||*

Call with avahan aadi panch mudra: *Aum vidurnamagnsi eha gocho...*

Do **panch upachar puja** of Viduragni

<u>**Udichyo home:**</u>
With shrub give ghee to Agni with these mantras and shed the remaining ghee on to the patrantar with *"edam"* mantra:

1. Vaam debya rishi anushtup chandau Agni Varunou devata prayaschitto home ey viniyogaha:
Tanno Agnebarunascho bidwan deboshyo hidho aba ya sishthana yajishtho bannitamam shosuchano biswan debana pramuh mugdhasmat swaha| Edam Agnivarunabyam

2. Vaam debya rishi anushtup chandau Agni Varuno devata prayaschitto home ey viniyoga ha:
Om tanno Agne habamo bhabhoti nedishtho ashya ushhso byushthou abajakshano Varunagnu barano brihi murikagu suhabo no edhi Swaha || Edam Agnivarunobyam|

3. Prajapati rishi bhritir chondou agni devata prayaschitto home ey viniyoghaha:
Aum ayaschagne shyanabhi shasti pascha satya mitwa maya asi| Aya no yajnam bahashya no dhehi bheshajagou swaha || Edam Agnaye

4. Aum Shunasefa rishi srishtup chandau Varunadayo devataha prayaschitto home ey viniyoga ha:
Aum yete shatang barunang ye sahasrang yajniya pasha bitota mahantaha, te bhirno adya Sabitota bishnur bishwe muchantwa marutang swarkaha Swaha ll
Edang Barunaya Sabitre Vishanave, biswebhyo devebhyo, marudoyo, swarkebhyo ||

5. Aum Sunasefa rishi srishtup chandau Varuna devata prayaschitto home ey viniyoga ha
Aum uduttamam Varuna pasham madbadhamang Bimadagnu shrekhayo | Atha Vaymadityo brate taba naga soaditaye syama swaha|| Edam Varunaya

Prayaschittyo homa sampoornam.

Other homas

Navagraha homa:
Aum Rabi grahaya swaha ,edam Rabi grahaya
Aum Soma grahaya swaha, edam Somo grahaya

Aum Mangal grahaya swaha, edam Mangal grahaya,
Aum Budh grahayaswaha, edam Budh grahaya,
Aum Brihaspatigrahaya swaha, edam Brihaspati grahaya
Aum Sukra grahaya swaha, edam Sukra grahaya,
Aum Shani grahaya swaha, edam Shani grahaya,
Aum Rahu grahaya swaha, edam Rahu grahaya,
Aum Ketu grahaya swaha, edam Ketu grahaya||

Dik palo homa: Have to be done in same pattern as Navagraha homa:
Indrayo, Agnayo, Yamayo, Nairutyayo, Barunayo Bayube Kuberaya, Eshanayo, Brahmanaya, Anantaya|
Ex. *Aum Indrayo swaha edam Indrayo.....*

Dash avatar: In similar manner:
Matsya avatara, Kurma avatara, Varaha avatara, Narasimha avatara, Vaman avatara, Parashuram avatara, Ram avatara, Balaram avatara, Krishna avatara, Buddha avatara, Kalki avatara|

Dash Maha Vidya: Similarly,
Kalikaoi, Taraoi, Shodashibhyo, Bhubhaneshwarai, Vairabyoi, Chinnamastaoi, Dhumavattai, Bagalaoi, Matangibhyo, Kamalatmikaoi|

Aum Pitha devataoi swaha| Edam Pitha devata||
Aum Kula devataoi swaha| Edam Kula devata||
Aum Istha devataoi swaha| Edam Istha devata||
Aum Sthane devataoi swaha| Edam Sthane devata||
Aum Pratyaksha devataya swaha| Edam Pratyaksha devata||

Aum Saraswattai swaha, Aum Suryay swaha, Aum agnaye swaha, Aum Shiva debyo swaha,Aum Durgaoi swaha, Aum Lakshmoi swaha, Aum Saraswattai swaha, Aum Brahmane swaha, Aum Vishnave swaha, Aum Narayanayo swaha, Aum Chatur vedayo swaha, Aum Hamshaoi swaha, Aum Saraswati aboharan devayo swaha, Aum Riddhi swaha, Aum Siddhi swaha, Aum Karthikaya swaha, Aum Radhikaya swaha, Aum Krishnayo swaha, Aum Kalikaoi swaha, Aum Gangaoi swaha, Aum Yamunaoi swaha, Aum Shitalaoi swaha, Aum Manashaoi swaha, Aum Ashoksundarioi swaha, Aum Naagrajaoi swaha, Aum Vastu purushayo swaha, Aum grammya dev debibyo swaha, Aum Dhanwantaribhyo swaha|

Purna-ahuti

Say: *Aum Agne twam Mriro namasi*

Do Dhyan of Agni: *Aum Pringa bhushma shruke shakshoha pinanga jatharo runaha| Chagastha saksho sutrognini saptarchi shakti dharakaha||*

Call Mriro-agni with avahan aadi panch mudra.

Do **panch upachar puja** of Mriro-agni.

Stand and play ghanta and other instruments for Agni and then lift the Arya-patra and give everything that is left in it to Agni with this mantra:

Aum murdhanang dibo arating prithibya boishbanaro mrito ajatam Agnim|
Kabigu samrajam tithignu jananam asanna patrang janayanta debaha swaha||

Show namaskar mudra:

Aum purnamadaha purnamidam purnat purna mudachyate, purnasya purnama dayo, poornamevaavashishyate||
Aum Shanti Aum Shanti Aum Shanti| Hari Aum tat sat||

Brahma dakshina

Sprinkle water on purna-patra: *Bong etoshmoing purna patra bhajyai namah*
Gandha-pushpa: *Ete gandha pushpe purna patra bhajyai namah*
Etot adhipate debayo Brahma Vishnu Maheshwaraya namaha
Sampradanayo purna patra bhajya Brahmane namaha

Utsarga: *Bishnurong tatsad adyo <month, paksha and tithi> tirthou Shri <name> <gotra> gotra karoyet Sri Saraswati pujanga bhutadom karmasargo tarthing dakshina midang purna-patra bhojjam Shri Vishnu daivatam mahchintang yatha sambhav gotro namne brahmane ahang samprade||*

Touch the bhajja on the Brahma and keep it to yourself.

Brahma Pranam: *Aum chatur badan samdastha chatur veda kutumbine| Dwijan ushtheyo sat karma sakshine Brahmane namah||*

Agni pranam

Aum twam Agnaye sarbabhutanam antascharisi pabaka, habang bahasi debanamataha shanting prayachame| Aum pringaksha lohita gribo protapingscho hutashon sakshi punya papang Dhananjay namastute||

Brahma visarjan

Shake the Brahma and put some curd on the south-east oF kund and say: *Aum Brahmanebhya khamasya|*

Agni Visarjan

Pour a mixture of curd and milk on Agni and say:
Aum Agne twam samudra gaccha|
Sprinkle water around the kund: *Aum Prithvi twam shitala bhawa|*

Yajna tilak

Pick up bhasma from Eshan (North east) direction into the patrantar and make tilak apply to Saraswati murthi:
Forehead: *Aum Kashapashya trayusham*
Neck: *Aum Yamad agne trayusham*
Shoulder: *Aum Yaddebanang trayusham*
Over the heart: *Aum tanneme yastu trayusham*

Apply the tilak to the ghat, Narayan, Self, Yajman and other devotees.

The Yajna is over.

Shri Saraswati Visarjan Vidhi

On the day of visarjan, these things have to be done if one wants to immerse their clay murthi into water:

1. Do normal puja and arati of panch devata and Saraswati
2. Do karo-suddhi as previously given
3. Touch the ghat and say: *"Aum Saraswattai khamasya"* for three times and *"Aum sarva deb debibhyo khamaddyam"* for three times.
4. Tear the string around the Ghat to make all dev/devi free from the Ghat.
5. Hold the ghat and shake it.
6. Stand on the right side of Saraswati and shake the murthi and say: *"Aum Saraswattai khamasya"* for three times and then shake the murthi of hangsha and say: *"Aum hangshaoi khamasya"* for three times.
7. **Pranam mantra:** *Aum gaccho gaccho param sthanang swasthano parameshwari sambatsyare vyatite tu punaragomoniay cha*||

Mantra visarjan is complete.

Now the murthi and ghat are to be carried to a water body with utmost devotion and then do pradakshina of the murthi and ghat for 3/7/9 times southwards and then immerse the murthi into water with Maa facing upwards.

Shri Shri Padma Puran-ukta Yajur vedio Shri Shri Saraswati Pooja Sampoornam

About the author

Ganapati puja Arati at IPGME&R and SSKM Hospital, 2023

Shri Shrav Banerjee, a medical student, passionately intertwines his academic pursuits with a profound commitment to the study and practice of Vedic rituals. With extensive experience guiding individuals on their spiritual journeys, he bridges ancient traditions with contemporary understanding. He is also the author of **Ekadantam Vidmahe**, a widely loved guide to Ganesh Pooja and Yajna. His deep interest in making age-old practices accessible to modern practitioners shines through in this comprehensive and heartfelt manual.